Peeking at PLANTS with a Scientist

Patricia J. Murphy

E **Enslow Publishers, Inc.**
40 Industrial Road   PO Box 38
Box 398   Aldershot
Berkeley Heights, NJ 07922   Hants GU12 6BP
USA   UK
http://www.enslow.com

Contents

Words to Know

botany (BAH tuh nee)—The study of plants.

botanist (BAH tuh nist)—Someone who studies plants.

disease (dih ZEEZ)—A sickness. Germs or viruses may cause disease.

fuel (FYOOL)—A material used to make power or heat.

medicine (MEH dih sin)—A drug that is used to treat a disease.

microscope (MYE kroh skohp)—An instrument that makes small objects or details look bigger.

Look around you. Plants are everywhere!

Many important things come from plants. Without plants, you could not live. The study of plants is called botany.

Botanists are scientists who study plants. They ask questions about plants.

Botanists use their eyes, ears, noses, and hands to learn more about plants. They look at plants. They smell and touch plants!

5

Meet Peter Raven.

He is a botanist. He runs the
Missouri Botanical Garden. The
garden is like a zoo for plants.

Scientist Peter teaches people to value all plants. He wants people to understand and take care of them.

Where do botanists work?

Some botanists work outdoors.
They may work in fields, forests,
or gardens.

Other botanists work indoors. They
may work in labs, offices, or schools.

A scientist looks at plant
samples in the lab.

How do botanists study plants?

Botanists gather plants from around the world. They look at the plants under microscopes. They store the plants in special books to keep them safe and dry.

Botanists put new facts about plants into computers. Computers and the Internet help botanists share these facts.

A plant sample should have flowers, fruits, and leaves. The plant is placed in newspaper and then dried.

How do botanists keep track of plants?

Botanists put plants into groups. Plants that are alike are put in the same group. These groups help botanists keep track of the world's plants.

There are over 350,000 types of plants.
Botanists find more every day.

13

What are the parts of a plant?

Most plants have flowers, leaves, stems, roots, and seeds. Food and wood come from these plant parts.

seeds

flowers

stems

leaves

roots

We eat grains, fruits, and vegetables.

We build houses with wood.

We use paper made of wood.

We wear clothes made of cotton.

Why do botanists study plants?

Botanists try to understand plants. Some botanists study why one plant grows better than another. This helps farmers grow bigger plants.

All plants need sunlight and water to grow.
Plants make their own food from sunlight.

17

How do botanists help people?

Some botanists study how people use plants. These scientists talk to people. They ask questions and read books. They learn which plants have been used for medicines.

The foxglove plant is used to make heart medicine.

Other botanists try to find new plants. The new plants may stop disease or become new fuels, clothes, foods, or other things.

Peter Raven started studying plants when he was six years old. He once found a plant that no one had seen in fifty years! Today, this plant's group name is *Ravenii*. It is named after him.

How many different plants can you find?

You will need:
- ✔ an adult
- ✔ a paper or cloth bag
- ✔ an outdoor area

Put inside your bag:
- ✔ a notebook and pencil
- ✔ scissors
- ✔ gardening gloves
- ✔ a hand lens (magnifying glass)
- ✔ tweezers
- ✔ plastic sandwich bags
- ✔ tape measure or ruler

1. Go outside with an adult. Draw pictures of the different plants you see. Put on your gardening gloves. Then, measure the plants. Use tweezers and scissors to collect small plant parts. Look at the parts with a hand lens. Put the parts in plastic bags.

2. Keep plant parts, drawings, and notes in your notebook. Ask questions like:

✔ What sizes, shapes, and colors are the plants?

✔ What kinds of plants did I find?

✔ How many types of plants did I find?

✔ Were any animals sitting on or eating the plants?

3. Visit the same area each season. Watch the plants change. Try to find new plants there. Search your neighborhood with an adult. Take your notebook on trips. Look around you. Plants are everywhere!

Books

Blevins, Wiley. *Parts of a Plant*. Minneapolis, Minn.: Compass Point Books, 2003.

Bocknek, Jonathan. *The Science of Plants*. Milwaukee, Wis.: Gareth Stevens, 1999.

Fowler, Allan. *From Seed to Plant*. Danbury, Conn.: Children's Press, 2001.

Ross, Michael Elsohn. *Flower Watching with Alice Eastwood*. Minneapolis, Minn.: Carolrhoda Books, 1997.

Whitehouse, Patricia. *Leaves*. Chicago, Ill.: Heinemann Library, 2002.

Web Sites

Missouri Botanical Garden. <http://www.mobot.org>

U. S. Department of Agriculture, Agricultural Research Service. *Sci4Kids*. "Plants." <http://www.ars.usda.gov/is/kids/plants/plantsintro.htm>

23

Index

❧ For my mother and father, who gave me roots, and still help me grow! ❧

Series Literacy Consultant:
Allan A. De Fina, Ph.D.
Past President of the New Jersey Reading Association
Professor, Department of Literacy Education
New Jersey City University

Science Consultant:
Peter Raven, Ph.D.
Director
Missouri Botanical Garden
St. Louis, Missouri

Note to Teachers and Parents: The **I Like Science!** series supports the National Science Education Standards for K–4 science, including content standards "Science as a human endeavor" and "Science as inquiry." The Words to Know section introduces subject-specific vocabulary, including pronunciation and definitions. Early readers may need help with these new words.

Library of Congress Cataloging-in-Publication Data

Murphy, Patricia J., 1963–
    Peeking at plants with a scientist / Patricia J. Murphy.
        p. cm. — (I like science!)
    Summary: Briefly explains the work of botanists, scientists who study different kinds of plants and how they work.
    ISBN 0-7660-2266-8 (hardcover)
    1. Botany—Juvenile literature. 2. Botanists—Juvenile literature. [1. Botany. 2. Botanists. 3. Plants.] I. Title. II. Series.

QK49.M97 2004
580-dc21

2003006805

Printed in the United States of America

10 9 8 7 6 5 4 3 2 1

To Our Readers: We have done our best to make sure all Internet Addresses in this book were active and appropriate when we went to press. However, the author and the publisher have no control over and assume no liability for the material available on those Internet sites or on other Web sites they may link to. Any comments or suggestions can be sent by e-mail to comments@enslow.com or to the address on the back cover.

Photo Credits: © 2002–2003 ArtToday, Inc., pp. 3, 7, 14, 15, 16, 17, 18; © Corel Corporation, p. 13; © Peter Taylor/Visuals Unlimited, pp. 5, 8; Photo courtesy of the Missouri Botanical Garden, pp. 4, 6, 9, 10, 11, 12, 20; United States Department of Agriculture, p. 19.

Cover Photo: © Peter Taylor/Visuals Unlimited